The Second World War

Conrad Mason

Designed by Karen Tomlins

History consultant: Terry Charman,
Imperial War Museum

Reading consultant: Alison Kelly,
Roehampton University

Edited by Jane Chisholm
Photographic manipulation by Keith Furnival

First published in 2010 by Usborne Publishing Ltd., Usborne House, 83-85 Saffron Hill, London
EC1N 8RT, England. www.usborne.com Copyright © 2010 Usborne Publishing Ltd.

Acknowledgements

© AKG-IMAGES pp20-21 (ullstein bild), p25(t), p29(b) (ullstein bild), p33(t), p47(l) (RIA Nowosti);
© ALAMY p7(b), p14(b) (Lebrecht Musica and Arts Photo Library), p19(t) (David Wall), p28(b)
(The Print Collector), p52(t) (akg-images), p58(t) (Trinity Mirror / Mirrorpix), p64 (Peter Titmuss),
p19(t) (Stephen Mulcahey), p47(r) (Serbia Pictures: Adam Radosavljevic); © THE ART ARCHIVE p1
(Stapleton Collection), p18(t) (Imperial War Museum / Eileen Tweedy), p30(b) (National Archives),
pp56-57 (Granger Collection); © BRIDGEMAN spine (Peter Newark Military Pictures), p40(t)
(SZ Photo); © CORBIS front cover (Hulton Deutsch Collection), pp4-5 (The Dmitri Baltermants
Collection), p13(t) (Hulton Deutsch Collection), pp22-23 (Bettmann), p35(t) (Georges de Keerle /
Sygma), p49(t) (Bettmann), pp52-53 (Yevgeny Khaldei), p59(m) (Bettmann), p61(b) (Bettmann),
pp62-63 (Bettmann); © GETTY IMAGES p4, p9 (Roger Viollet), p8(b), p10(t) (Popperfoto), p12(b)
(Popperfoto), p16(b) (Time & Life Pictures), pp24-25(b), pp32-33(b), p37(m), pp38-39(b), p44(b)
(Hulton Archive / Archive Photos), p48(t) (AFP); © IMPERIAL WAR MUSEUM, LONDON pp2-3 (H
1656), p5(t) (GER_530), p17(r) (HU 3266), p19(b) (HU 49833), p26(b) (IWM ART LD 5620), p31(b)
(NYF 42432), pp34-35 (MH 9701), p38(l) (E 18980), pp42-43 (EA 51048), p45(t) (HU 3349), p45(b)
(MH 27178), p46(b) (HU 56936), p48(b) (IWM MH 2111B), p50(t) (EA 48572), pp54-55(b) (NYP
59700), p55(t) (MH 2629); © TOPFOTO back cover (Topham Picturepoint), p7(t) (Roger-Viollet),
pp36-37 (Topham Picturepoint), p51(b) (Lightroom Photos)

Title page: Members of the Hitler Youth march
through a stadium in Nuremberg, Germany in 1933.

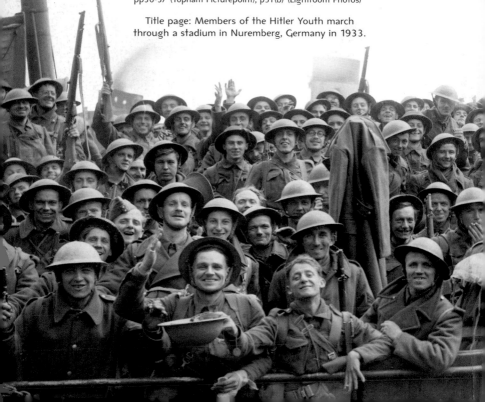

Contents

British troops crammed
on the deck of a warship
in May 1940

Peace for our time

On a chilly September day in 1938, Neville Chamberlain, the British Prime Minister, delivered a speech in London. Many of those who gathered to listen were uneasy. They feared that a terrible war was about to break out in Europe. But the Prime Minister, who had just returned from Germany, brought a message of hope.

"I believe it is peace for our time," he declared. "I recommend you to go home and sleep quietly in your beds."

Neville Chamberlain waves an agreement, signed by himself and Adolf Hitler, ruler of Germany, which he thought was proof that there would be "peace for our time."

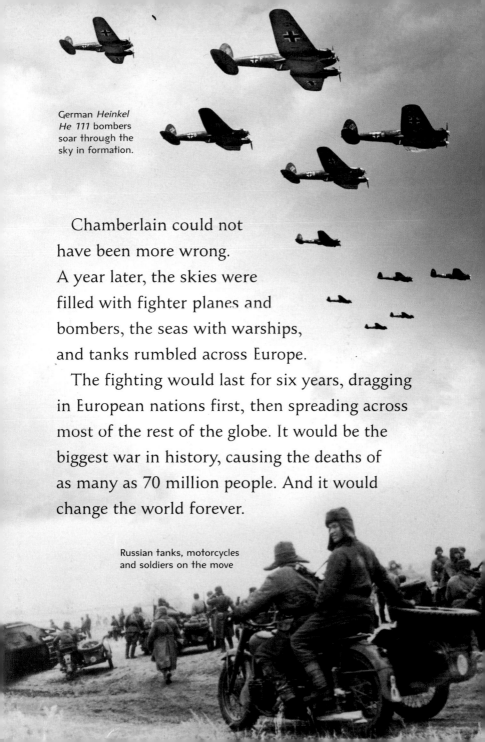

German *Heinkel He 111* bombers soar through the sky in formation.

Chamberlain could not have been more wrong. A year later, the skies were filled with fighter planes and bombers, the seas with warships, and tanks rumbled across Europe.

The fighting would last for six years, dragging in European nations first, then spreading across most of the rest of the globe. It would be the biggest war in history, causing the deaths of as many as 70 million people. And it would change the world forever.

Russian tanks, motorcycles and soldiers on the move

Chapter 1
The rise of Hitler

At the start of the 1920s, the people of Europe were recovering from the First World War. This long, bloody struggle had ended in 1918, with Britain, France and the USA victorious over Germany, Austria-Hungary and their allies.

But although the war was over, the Germans were still suffering. They had to pay huge fines called 'reparations' to the victors. This was especially hard as their government had spent a fortune trying to win the war, leaving the economy in ruins.

Things went from bad to worse. The value of German money dropped, until it was so worthless that children played with bundles of cash as toys. At one point, it was said that you needed a wheelbarrow full of money to buy a loaf of bread.

Then, in 1929, the US stock market crashed. This sparked the Great Depression – a time of poverty and unemployment which spread all over the world, and hit Germany particularly badly.

German children play games with worthless money.

In these desperate times, a man named
Adolf Hitler rose to power. He promised
to save the nation from poverty, while
threatening and bullying his opponents.
By 1934, he was all-powerful in
Germany, ruling the nation
as a dictator.

Adolf Hitler usually wore
a military-style uniform
in public. Here, he is
delivering a special salute,
which became the
official greeting
in Germany.

Hitler had factories and motorways built, which created new jobs. He also strengthened the armed forces. At last, many Germans felt that they could take pride in their country again.

But their new ruler was a dangerous man, full of hatred. He was the leader of a party called the National Socialists, nicknamed the Nazis. They were racists, who believed that Jewish people were responsible for all the problems in Germany.

Hitler's men murdered his political opponents, and persecuted Jews, Gypsies and Slavs. To the Nazis, these people weren't people at all. They were *untermensch* – sub-human.

These Nazi troopers are standing outside a Jewish shop, stopping anyone from going in. The placard says, "Don't buy from Jews."

Like most Germans, Hitler believed that his country had been treated badly after the First World War. In fiery speeches, he demanded justice, and more *Lebensraum* – living space – for the German people. There was only one way to get this living space, and that was war.

Adolf Hitler was an energetic and talented public speaker. On his left arm he wears a black Swastika – the symbol of the Nazi Party.

Most European governments were suspicious of Hitler, but he did have one ally. Benito Mussolini, *Il Duce* (meaning 'the boss') of Italy, was a dictator too. He shared many of Hitler's ideas, and wanted to create an Italian empire.

These two terrifying men decided to take the land they wanted by force. Mussolini invaded Ethiopia. Hitler sent troops into German land on the border of France – an action which was forbidden by a treaty signed after the First World War. Then he sent troops into Austria, and united it with Germany.

There were protests from the League of Nations – a worldwide organization set up to keep the peace. But Hitler and Mussolini just ignored them.

This map shows the land taken over by Hitler during the 1930s.

Memel
(March
1939)

Germany
in 1930

Land taken over
during 1930s,
with dates
occupied

GERMANY

Sudetenland
(September 1938)

Bohemia and Moravia
(March 1939)

CZECHOSLOVAKIA

Rhineland
(March
1936)

AUSTRIA
(March
1938)

Neville Chamberlain inspects some of Hitler's troops, on a visit to Germany.

Politicians in Britain and France were alarmed. Some felt they had a duty to protect nations that were under threat. But most were prepared to do anything to avoid another war. These politicians tried to 'appease' Hitler by letting him take what he wanted, in the hope that he would soon stop.

In September 1938, the British and French governments allowed Hitler to take over part of Czechoslovakia. In return, Hitler promised that this was the last claim on territory that he would make. Throughout Europe there was relief. There would be peace after all.

Unfortunately, Hitler was lying. In March 1939, his soldiers occupied most of the rest of Czechoslovakia – and even then, he wasn't satisfied. As dawn broke on September 1, German forces surged into Poland without warning.

The British and French had promised to protect Poland. But Hitler thought that they were mere 'worms' who would never dare stand up to him.

This time, he was wrong. With a heavy heart, Neville Chamberlain made a radio broadcast to the British people. "This country," he announced, "is at war with Germany."

These British children are leaving their homes in London to live in the countryside, in case the city is bombed.

German troops
advance to attack
a Polish post office
in Danzig.

Chapter 2

Blitzkrieg

In the First World War, soldiers had fought in
muddy trenches, struggling for years over a small
stretch of land. This time, Hitler decided that
things would be different. This time, he would
win by *Blitzkrieg*, meaning 'lightning warfare'.

In the first week of September, German planes
swooped over Poland, bombing factories and
military buildings. Meanwhile, German troops
advanced rapidly, with motorcycles and tanks,
toward the Polish capital – Warsaw. The idea
was to shock the defending forces into surrender
as fast as possible.

The Poles were taken completely by surprise. They had a large army, but it was badly equipped. Some soldiers even rode into battle on horseback, armed with lances. In less than a month, Hitler's *Blitzkrieg* had brought Poland to its knees.

The British and French were dismayed. But things were about to get even worse – Russian soldiers joined the attack on Poland.

The Russians had fought against Germany in the First World War. But, since then, the old Russian Empire had become the Soviet Union. It was a Communist state, which meant that it was supposed to be ruled by the people. But in fact it was ruled by an all-powerful dictator – a man called Joseph Stalin.

A portrait of Joseph Stalin, dictator of the Soviet Union

British and French politicians had suspected that Stalin wanted more land for the Soviet Union, and they were right. He and Hitler carved up Poland between them, and the next year, his troops occupied Estonia, Latvia and Lithuania.

Meanwhile, Hitler turned his army around, and brought *Blitzkrieg* to western Europe. Here, too, it was a wild success. In a matter of weeks, his troops had stormed through Denmark, Norway, the Netherlands, Belgium...

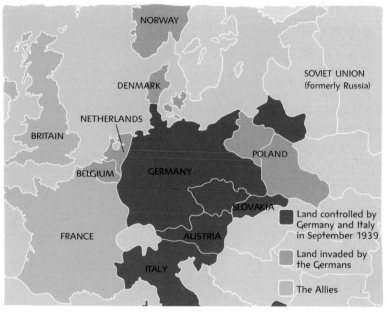

This map shows how far Hitler's army had advanced by early May 1940.

Despite declaring war, the British and French, known as the Allies, had done almost nothing to stop Hitler. But now they had to fight – because the next country he planned to invade was France.

The Allies thought they were ready. After the First World War, the French had built a colossal network of fortifications – the Maginot Line – along the border with Germany. By spring 1940, a large part of their army was defending

The Maginot Line only covered the French border with Germany.

this line. Meanwhile, a small British force had landed in northern France, and was positioned along the border with Belgium.

But the Allies had underestimated Hitler. A cunning commander, he decided to attack from Belgium, through the wooded Ardennes region, where there was no Maginot Line to hold him back. This meant he could split the Allied forces in two.

German soldiers charge through a French village in May 1940.

As German tanks thundered into France, British troops found themselves trapped to the north of the Ardennes. Sensing disaster, the British government sent a fleet of ships to ferry their men home from the port of Dunkirk.

Meanwhile, French forces fought desperately to hold off the Germans. But soon it was all over. Paris was captured on June 14, 1940.

In the First World War, the Allies had defended France for four years. This time, they had lasted just four weeks.

Hitler visited France soon after its defeat. He insisted on receiving the official French surrender in the same railway carriage in which the Germans had surrendered at the end of the First World War.

In Britain, people realized they would be next. But their new Prime Minister, Winston Churchill, was defiant.

"We shall fight on the beaches," he told the nation. "We shall fight on the landing grounds, we shall fight in the fields and in the streets. We shall fight in the hills. We shall never surrender."

Winston Churchill appears on a poster, encouraging the British to resist Hitler.

Hitler knew that invading Britain wasn't going to be easy. It could only be reached by sky or sea, and the British navy was one of the strongest in the world. So, German commanders decided that their air force, the *Luftwaffe*, would bomb Britain into submission. Then their army would invade.

The Battle of Britain began with German bombers striking British airfields, day and night. But they hadn't counted on the fierce resistance of Britain's Royal Air Force. RAF pilots struggled

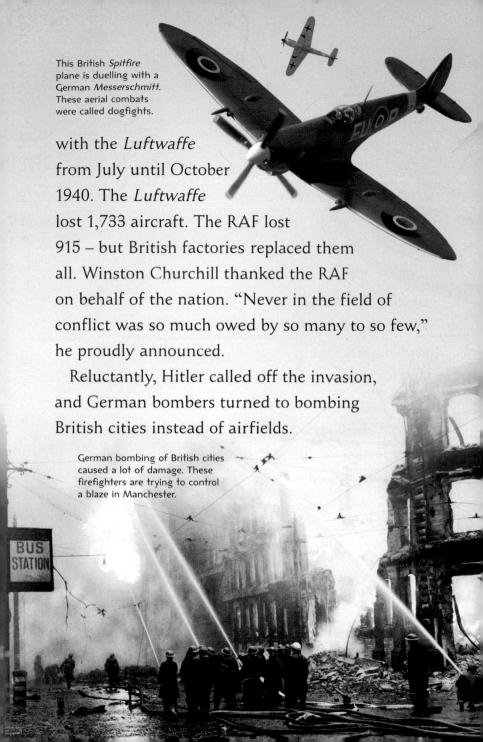

This British *Spitfire* plane is duelling with a German *Messerschmitt*. These aerial combats were called dogfights.

with the *Luftwaffe* from July until October 1940. The *Luftwaffe* lost 1,733 aircraft. The RAF lost 915 – but British factories replaced them all. Winston Churchill thanked the RAF on behalf of the nation. "Never in the field of conflict was so much owed by so many to so few," he proudly announced.

Reluctantly, Hitler called off the invasion, and German bombers turned to bombing British cities instead of airfields.

German bombing of British cities caused a lot of damage. These firefighters are trying to control a blaze in Manchester.

BUS
STATION

The Battle of Britain was a setback for Hitler. But elsewhere he was enjoying more success. In April 1941, his forces helped Mussolini's army to conquer Greece and Yugoslavia. In May, German troops captured Crete. That meant that Germany and Italy now controlled almost all of Europe.

Hitler's ambitions didn't stop there, though. Joseph Stalin had worked with Hitler to invade Poland, and was supplying Germany with oil, tin and rubber, to fuel vehicles and make weapons. But the truth was that Hitler hated the Russians, and hated Communism. So, on June 22, 1941, he launched Operation Barbarossa – a campaign to conquer the Soviet Union.

This map shows German and Italian domination of Europe, before the attack on Russia.

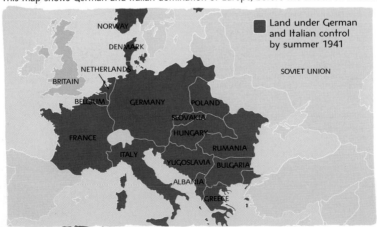

Land under German and Italian control by summer 1941

NORWAY

DENMARK

NETHERLANDS

BRITAIN

BELGIUM   GERMANY   POLAND

SLOVAKIA

HUNGARY

FRANCE

ITALY

YUGOSLAVIA   BULGARIA

ALBANIA

GREECE

RUMANIA

SOVIET UNION

Hitler sent thousands of tanks into the Soviet Union. Soon, they were deep inside Russia, and advancing towards the capital, Moscow.

Just as before, German troops advanced across the border in a *Blitzkrieg* attack. And, just as before, they forced the defenders back. It looked as if the invasion would be another easy victory.

Hitler was sure that if the Soviet Union fell, the war would be over. But, even as his troops marched further and further east, things were rapidly spinning out of his control. Events far away, in the Pacific Ocean, had turned the European war into a world war.

Chapter 3

The tiger and the bear

Pearl Harbor is a United States naval base on the tropical island of Oahu, in the Pacific Ocean. On the morning of December 7, 1941, American battleships were lying at anchor there, when planes screamed out of the skies towards them.

Within minutes, the ships were torn apart by bombs and machine-gun fire. By the end of the morning, nearly 200 US planes and vessels had been lost, and over 2,000 people were dead.

The planes that attacked Pearl Harbor belonged to the Japanese. In late 1940, they had signed a tripartite (three-way) pact with Germany and Italy, forming the Axis Powers.

Like Hitler and Mussolini, the Japanese government wanted to create an empire. But before they could take over nearby islands

in the Pacific Ocean and southeast Asia, they needed to smash the US navy. It was among the most powerful in the world, and might stand in the way of Japanese conquests.

The Japanese had attacked without declaring war, and the Americans were furious. American Admiral Halsey visited Pearl Harbor soon after the raid. "Before we're through with this," he muttered, "the Japanese language will be spoken only in hell."

US President Roosevelt gave a speech, calling December 7, "a date which will live in infamy." An hour later, the USA declared war on Japan. By the end of the week, it had joined the Allies and was at war with all the Axis Powers.

US warships ablaze at Pearl Harbor. The ship on the right is the *USS Arizona,* on which a thousand men were killed.

In Britain, Winston Churchill and his government were delighted. The Americans had been lending them money and selling them weapons since just after the start of the war, but that wasn't enough.

A large part of the British army was stuck in the deserts of North Africa, struggling against a combined German and Italian force. The Germans were led by Erwin Rommel, a brilliant tank commander nicknamed the 'Desert Fox'. His forces weren't as strong as those of the British, but he still managed to run circles around them, striking fast and disappearing just as quickly.

British soldiers watch German vehicles burning in the desert, after a lightning-quick raid by Erwin Rommel's forces.

This photograph was taken from a U-boat. It shows a British steamship that has just been hit by the U-boat's torpedoes.

Even at sea, where the British navy had always been successful, things were going badly. In the Atlantic Ocean, British supply ships were being attacked and sunk by German submarines, called U-boats. This meant that the British were suffering from shortages of food and equipment.

The USA had joined the war just in time – Britain desperately needed help.

Meanwhile, the Japanese government took advantage of their success at Pearl Harbor to start building the empire they longed for. Their troops overran nearby islands and swathes of territory in the Far East, including the British colonies of Hong Kong, Malaya and Singapore.

During these invasions, Japanese soldiers won a reputation for ferocity. They fought harder than any of their opponents, and never gave up. They believed that anyone who surrendered was weak and cowardly, so they treated prisoners with brutal contempt, even if they were civilians. Many were fed poorly, and died of starvation.

This painting shows British women and children, captured during the Japanese invasion of Singapore. On the floor is a bathtub of rice – their food for the day.

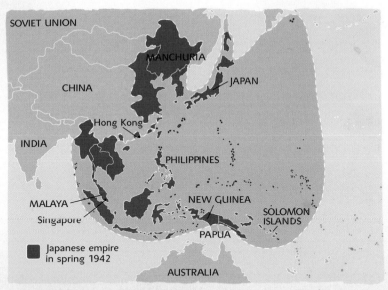

This map shows 'The Greater East Asian Co-Prosperity Sphere' – the Japanese empire.

As well as taking prisoners, the Japanese massacred thousands of innocent people, to show others that there was no point in resisting. Sometimes, they even forced local people to bury their murdered friends and family.

But, despite their victories, many Japanese generals and politicians were nervous. Admiral Yamamoto, who masterminded the attack on Pearl Harbor, knew the Americans would strike back. "I fear we have only succeeded in awakening a sleeping tiger," he warned his countrymen.

Yamamoto wasn't the only Axis commander to be concerned. German generals in Russia were having far more trouble than they'd expected.

Their army's progress was painfully slow, as Russian roads were mostly dirt tracks, and distances between cities were vast. Every step of the way, they faced resistance from local peasants. Old men, women and children attacked the Germans with any weapons they could get hold of, desperate to drive the invaders out of their homelands. The Soviet land forces, known as the Red Army, burned crops when they retreated, so that the Germans couldn't use them.

A German soldier advances past a burning Russian farmhouse.

It was becoming clear that the invasion of Russia was going to be a long slog, nothing like the speedy victories that Hitler had enjoyed in Europe. This was confirmed when the Germans tried to capture the city of Leningrad in September 1941. They ended up stuck in a siege that dragged on, month after month, with no end in sight.

The armies of the Axis Powers had conquered vast areas of the globe. But how long could they cling on to their new possessions? They would soon find out. The American tiger and the Russian bear were about to bite back.

This German magazine shows Joseph Stalin and Russia, as a large bear. Russia was often shown as a bear in cartoons, because it was so vast.

Chapter 4
Fighting back

In May 1942, American codebreakers intercepted some Japanese radio messages, which revealed that Admiral Yamamoto was planning to invade New Guinea. US admirals quickly made plans to ambush his fleet in the Coral Sea, off the north-eastern coast of Australia.

It was the first sea battle in history in which neither fleet saw each other. The fighting was done by planes, launched from aircraft carriers – massive floating fortresses with runways on deck.

In the end, it wasn't a great victory for the Americans, but it did stop the invasion. Yamamoto realized he had to beat the US navy as soon as possible. So he decided to attack the American island

A plane prepares to take off from an aircraft carrier. These planes had folding wings, so they could be stored side-by-side.

of Midway, which lay right in the middle of the Pacific Ocean. This would lure US aircraft carriers into a final battle, where they could be destroyed.

The plan worked – but not in the way Yamamoto had hoped. The Americans intercepted his messages again, so they knew the exact location of the Japanese ships. On June 4, US planes swooped down to bomb the enemy vessels, and managed to destroy four of the Japanese navy's ten carriers.

The Battle of Midway was one of the greatest Allied victories of the war. In a single day, the Americans broke the power of the Japanese fleet, and won control of the Pacific Ocean. But liberating the islands that the Japanese had conquered would prove to be a lot more difficult.

Japanese fighter planes attack US ships at the Battle of Midway.

Meanwhile, in Russia, German forces were closing in on the city of Stalingrad. The defending troops were outnumbered, and Hitler was confident that they would soon surrender. This would allow his forces to take control of large oilfields that lay to the south of Stalingrad.

Sure enough, the Germans captured most of the city, pushing back the defenders and smashing whole streets to rubble with their gunfire. But the Russians stubbornly refused to give up, and many of them chose to die rather than let their city fall into German hands.

One Russian soldier wrote a defiant message on the wall of the Stalingrad railway station: "General Rodimtsev's guardsmen fought and died here for their motherland."

At Stalingrad, Russian troops were under orders to 'hug the enemy'. This meant they stayed as close to the Germans as possible, so that German planes couldn't attack them without hitting their own troops.

This Russian woman is trying to cook dinner in the ruins of her house, while the Battle of Stalingrad rages on around her.

Ruined buildings protected the Russian defenders from enemy bullets, and German tanks were useless in the narrow streets. The fighting got more and more bloody, and tens of thousands of civilians were killed.

Winter came, and parts of Stalingrad still held out. It was bitterly cold and snowy, and the German soldiers shivered in uniforms that weren't warm enough. Worse – for them – Russian reinforcements had begun to arrive. In December, they marched around the outskirts of the city, surrounding the invaders.

The German commander, Paulus, realized how desperate the situation was. He begged Hitler to let him retreat, but Hitler refused.

By February 1943, the Germans were trapped, frozen and starving, and Paulus himself was captured. With no hope of escape, the remaining German troops finally surrendered to the Red Army. They were sent to Soviet prison camps, where most of them died of disease or starvation.

Field Marshal Friedrich Paulus

Hitler was furious, and began feverishly looking for a chance to turn the tables on Stalin's army. But time was against him. Every day, the British and Americans were sending supplies to Russia, while Russian factories were churning out more tanks and equipment, making the Red Army stronger and stronger. Hitler had to attack soon. The only question was, where?

These Rumanian soldiers, allies of the Germans, are being taken to prison camps deep in the Soviet Union.

In the end, he decided on the area around the Russian city of Kursk. There were German forces to the north and south of the city, so they could attack from both sides at once. Hitler began gathering troops and tanks for a vast battle – one that he believed would win the war, or lose it. "A victory at Kursk," he told his generals, "would shine like a beacon to the world."

Unfortunately for him, the Russians guessed where he was going to attack, and built up strong defensive lines and minefields. When the Germans finally struck, the Russians were ready for them.

The fighting raged for days, through pouring rain. The German army proved as deadly as ever, killing tens of thousands of enemy soldiers, and wrecking many hundreds of tanks. But the Soviet

Soviet *T-34* tanks attack at the Battle of Kursk. These vehicles were among the best tanks of the war, and were also cheap to produce.

forces were too large to defeat, and their defensive lines were too strong. Frustrated, German commanders had to call off the attack.

Hitler had underestimated the Soviet Union, and now he was going to pay for it. Slowly but surely, the sprawling Red Army began its own advance – towards Berlin.

During the Battle of Kursk, a German soldier despairs next to the wreckage of an artillery gun, and the body of a comrade.

Chapter 5

Into Europe

As Hitler's troops began battling for Stalingrad, a new British commander had arrived in North Africa. His name was Bernard Montgomery, but to his men he was known as 'Monty'.

Led by the energetic Monty, the British finally managed to beat the 'Desert Fox' – the German commander Rommel – at a place called El Alamein, in late 1942. It was the first big British victory on land against the Germans.

Lieutenant-General Montgomery watches the Germans retreat during the Battle of El Alamein.

Rommel was running out of fuel and supplies, and when American troops landed in North Africa, he found himself surrounded. Just as Paulus had done, he asked Hitler for permission to get his men out. But, once again, Hitler wouldn't

The Axis and the Allies fought battles all along the coastline of North Africa.

hear of it, and told Rommel that "victory or death" were his only options. On May 13, 1943, Rommel's men chose to surrender instead, leaving the Allies masters of North Africa.

Most of the German army was still tied up in Russia, so the Allied commanders seized this opportunity to attack Italy – the 'soft underbelly' of Europe, as Churchill liked to call it.

Italian troops run for cover at the Battle of El Alamein, as British guns fire explosive shells at them.

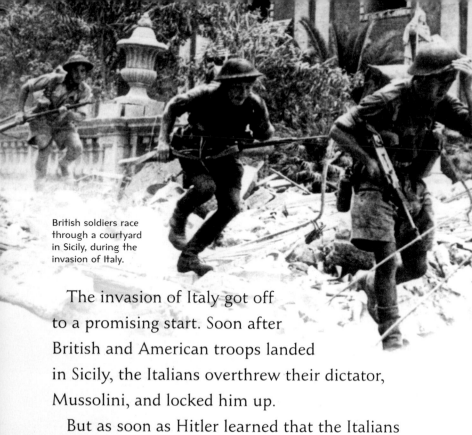

British soldiers race through a courtyard in Sicily, during the invasion of Italy.

The invasion of Italy got off to a promising start. Soon after British and American troops landed in Sicily, the Italians overthrew their dictator, Mussolini, and locked him up.

But as soon as Hitler learned that the Italians were planning to make peace, he ordered German forces in Italy to take over, set up defensive lines and fight off the Allies. He also sent an élite squad of German soldiers to rescue Mussolini. They landed gliders next to the hotel where *Il Duce* was imprisoned, and flew him to safety.

American and British forces began a slow struggle north, towards the Italian capital – Rome.

Meanwhile, the Allies were planning an even bigger invasion. Ever since the retreat from Dunkirk, they had been gathering troops in Britain, for 'D-Day' – the day when they would return to liberate France. Americans and Canadians flooded in. There were Polish, French, Dutch, Belgian and Czech troops too, all eager to free their homes. By June 1944, the invasion force was vast. Finally, the Allies were ready.

Hitler guessed that they were going to attack – but he didn't know where. So, to fool him, the British built up fake supply dumps and a fake invasion fleet opposite the French port of Calais. The real plan was to land on the beaches of Normandy, which weren't so well defended.

The attack was planned for June 5. But a few days before, a storm blew up at sea, and the whole operation had to be put on hold. Allied soldiers waited anxiously, unsure what was going to happen.

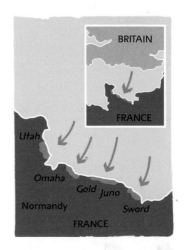

The Allied commanders chose five beaches in Normandy for the invasion. Each one had its own codename, as shown on this map.

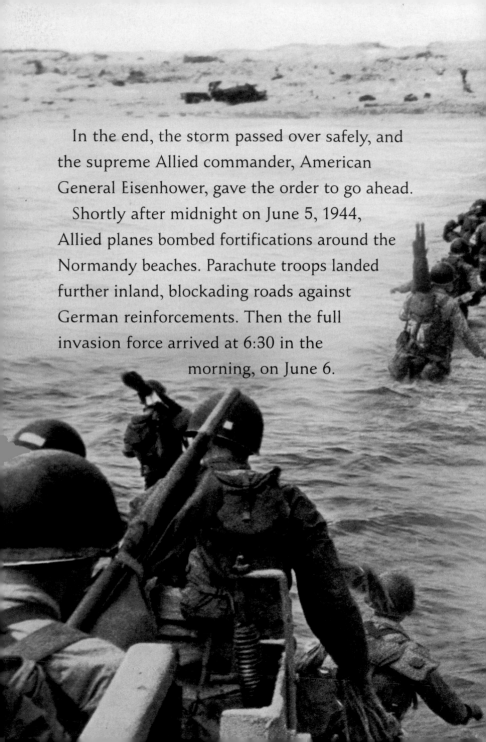

In the end, the storm passed over safely, and the supreme Allied commander, American General Eisenhower, gave the order to go ahead.

Shortly after midnight on June 5, 1944, Allied planes bombed fortifications around the Normandy beaches. Parachute troops landed further inland, blockading roads against German reinforcements. Then the full invasion force arrived at 6:30 in the morning, on June 6.

US soldiers disembark from their landing craft to attack *Utah* beach.

The Germans were taken by surprise, and most of the beaches were badly defended. There was fierce fighting in some areas, and by the end of the day, 2,500 Allied soldiers had been killed. But over 150,000 had made it ashore. Over the next month, more and more Allied troops poured into France, ready to drive Hitler's forces back towards Germany.

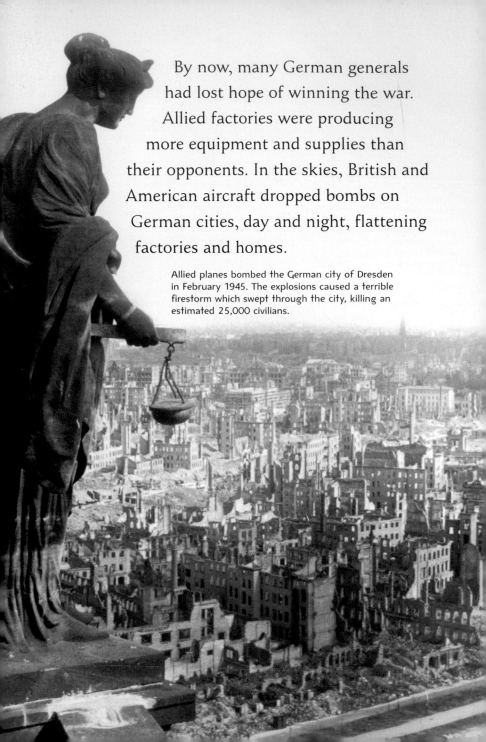

By now, many German generals had lost hope of winning the war. Allied factories were producing more equipment and supplies than their opponents. In the skies, British and American aircraft dropped bombs on German cities, day and night, flattening factories and homes.

Allied planes bombed the German city of Dresden in February 1945. The explosions caused a terrible firestorm which swept through the city, killing an estimated 25,000 civilians.

An Allied convoy steams across the North Sea, with a cargo of coal.

At sea, Allied supply ships sailed in convoys, protected by plenty of warships – which made it very difficult for the German U-boats to sink them.

The Allies also had a secret advantage. In 1941, the British had found an *Enigma* machine in a captured U-boat. This was a German device used to transmit coded messages. A team of codebreakers managed to crack the *Enigma* codes, so the Allies were able to read the Germans' secret messages, and find out what their plans were. The Germans had no idea that the codes had been broken.

The *Enigma* machine scrambled up the letters in a message, so that it could only be decoded using another *Enigma* machine.

As the Allies advanced through France, the Nazi empire began to fall apart. Hitler had exploited defeated nations, taking food and supplies for his troops, and forcing civilians to leave their homes and families to work in factories in Germany, making weapons for the German army.

Every day, more and more of these people fought back by passing on secret information to the Allies, or even attacking German bases and trains. They knew that if they were caught they could be tortured or executed. But they were still determined to fight for freedom.

This Frenchman is laying explosives on a railway line used by the Germans.

Some of these men and women later became known as heroes because of their bravery. In 1942, one Yugoslavian resistance fighter, Stjepan Filipovic, was about to be hanged by the Nazis when he threw out his arms and yelled, "Freedom to the people!"

Today, Filipovic's bravery before he was hanged is commemorated by a statue.

Filipovic's wish came true after his death. In October 1944, a band of Yugoslavians, led by Josip Tito, captured the nation's capital, Belgrade, and drove out the Germans.

On July 20, 1944, a brave German, Colonel von Stauffenberg, even tried to assassinate Hitler. He and several other officers hoped to take control of Germany and make peace with the Allies.

Colonel von Stauffenberg, would-be assassin of Hitler

Stauffenberg planted a bomb in Hitler's headquarters – the 'Wolf's Lair'. But when the bomb went off, Hitler was only injured. Stauffenberg was executed, along with the officers who had helped him.

The Nazis weren't beaten yet. As the winter of 1944 approached, the Axis Powers launched more furious attacks, aiming to turn the tables on the Allies.

Mussolini and Hitler inspect the damage caused by the bomb in the Wolf's Lair.

A Japanese *kamikaze* pilot is shot down by anti-aircraft guns as he tries to crash into a US aircraft carrier.

Chapter 6

Victory

In October 1944, the Japanese gathered together every ship they could find, and attacked the US navy in the Pacific Ocean. The two fleets clashed at Leyte Gulf, in the biggest sea battle in history. It lasted three days, but once again the American fleet proved stronger.

In desperation, many Japanese pilots carried out *kamikaze* attacks – they loaded their planes with explosives and flew straight into enemy ships, killing themselves in the process.

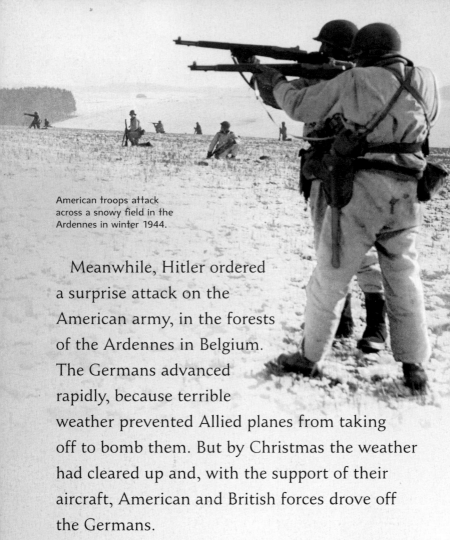

American troops attack across a snowy field in the Ardennes in winter 1944.

Meanwhile, Hitler ordered a surprise attack on the American army, in the forests of the Ardennes in Belgium. The Germans advanced rapidly, because terrible weather prevented Allied planes from taking off to bomb them. But by Christmas the weather had cleared up and, with the support of their aircraft, American and British forces drove off the Germans.

Now an Allied victory was just a matter of time. British and American troops pushed into Germany from the west, while the Red Army closed in from the east.

As they did so, the Allies uncovered the awful truth of Hitler's rule. British war correspondent Richard Dimbleby was with British soldiers when they stumbled on a large camp, known as Belsen, near the town of Bergen in Germany. What they found inside horrified them. "Over an acre of ground lay dead and dying people," Dimbleby reported. "You could not see which was which."

It was one of many concentration camps, set up as prisons for Jews. The Nazis had locked up as many as they could lay hands on. Then, from 1941 onwards, they had begun to kill them, mostly with poison gas. News of this mass murder, now known as the Holocaust, shocked the world.

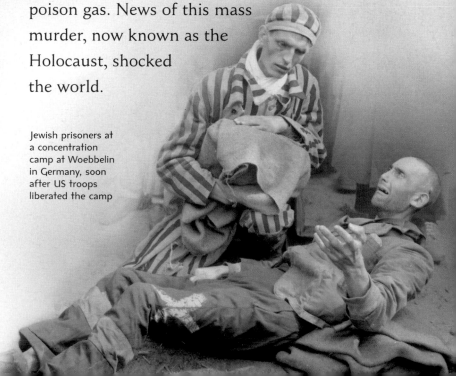

Jewish prisoners at a concentration camp at Woebbelin in Germany, soon after US troops liberated the camp

This painting shows Soviet tanks rolling into Berlin. In the distance is the Brandenburg Gate, the city's most iconic monument.

Realizing that the end was near, Hitler retreated to an underground bunker in Berlin. He ordered factories, hospitals and power stations to be destroyed, so that they couldn't fall into the Allies' hands.

By April 1945, the Russians had reached Berlin, and began hunting down the tattered remnants of the German army in the streets.

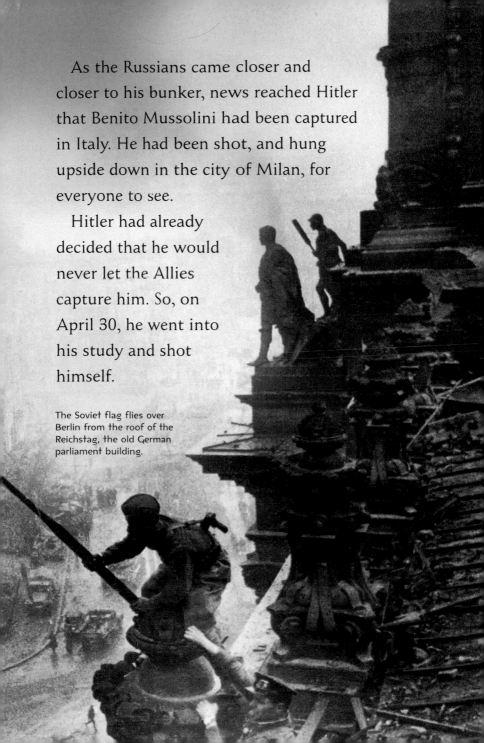

As the Russians came closer and closer to his bunker, news reached Hitler that Benito Mussolini had been captured in Italy. He had been shot, and hung upside down in the city of Milan, for everyone to see.

Hitler had already decided that he would never let the Allies capture him. So, on April 30, he went into his study and shot himself.

The Soviet flag flies over Berlin from the roof of the Reichstag, the old German parliament building.

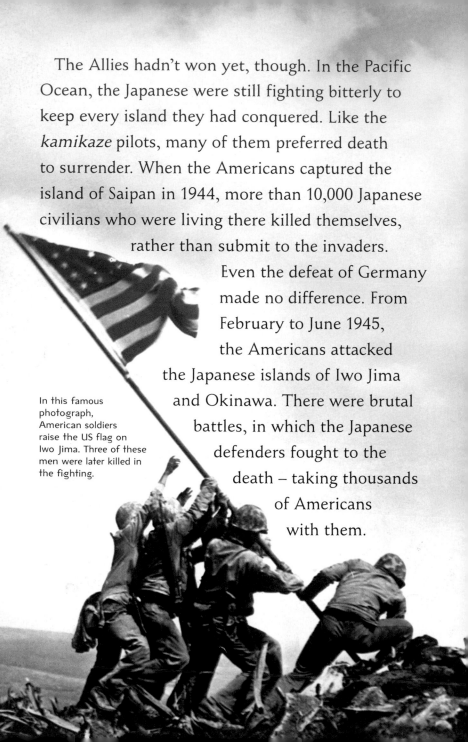

The Allies hadn't won yet, though. In the Pacific Ocean, the Japanese were still fighting bitterly to keep every island they had conquered. Like the *kamikaze* pilots, many of them preferred death to surrender. When the Americans captured the island of Saipan in 1944, more than 10,000 Japanese civilians who were living there killed themselves, rather than submit to the invaders.

Even the defeat of Germany made no difference. From February to June 1945, the Americans attacked the Japanese islands of Iwo Jima and Okinawa. There were brutal battles, in which the Japanese defenders fought to the death – taking thousands of Americans with them.

In this famous photograph, American soldiers raise the US flag on Iwo Jima. Three of these men were later killed in the fighting.

It seemed as if the Japanese would never give up. But, in the summer of 1945, the Americans tested out a new secret weapon, which they believed would force Japan to surrender. It was called the atomic bomb.

The atomic bomb produced a vast amount of smoke, known as a mushroom cloud because of its shape.

The bomb was developed by a team of Allied scientists, led by J. Robert Oppenheimer. If it worked, it would be more powerful than any weapon the world had ever seen. It would be able to wipe out a city in a single blast.

In the deserts of New Mexico, a test bomb was detonated. It was a success. Oppenheimer was filled with awe at what he had done. He remembered a line from a Hindu poem which summed up his feelings – "Now I am become Death, the destroyer of worlds."

The Americans produced two atomic bombs, codenamed *Little Boy* and *Fat Man*. In August, they dropped *Little Boy* on the Japanese city of Hiroshima, then *Fat Man* on the city of Nagasaki.

The results were horrific. Vast, billowing clouds rose into the sky, hiding the destruction beneath. When the smoke cleared, Hiroshima and Nagasaki were barren, desolate wastelands, almost unrecognizable as cities.

This photograph shows the city of Hiroshima, devastated after the atomic bomb explosion.

The two explosions were to kill over 300,000 people between them. Those close to the blasts were instantly burned to death. Others were crushed by falling buildings, choked on smoke, or died months or years later of burns or radiation poisoning, a sickness caused by atomic explosions.

The atomic bomb was by far the most destructive weapon ever created, and now that the Americans knew its secret, the world would never be the same again. The Japanese government's only option was to admit defeat. On September 2, 1945, they formally surrendered. Six long years after it began, the Second World War was finally over.

Members of the British WRENS (Women's Royal Naval Service) celebrate victory in Brighton, England.

Chapter 7

Aftermath

At last, there was peace. But while many celebrated, some saw it as their chance to take violent revenge. In Berlin, Soviet soldiers ran wild, ransacking homes, assaulting women, rounding up Nazi officials and shooting them. In every country that the Germans had occupied, those who had helped the invaders were publicly humiliated, imprisoned, executed or murdered.

In the following months, order was restored. Hitler's closest henchmen were put on trial at Nuremberg, a German city where the Nazis had held large parades. Some of these men were hanged. Others killed themselves before they could be brought to justice.

Members of the Nazi regime on trial at Nuremberg. The man in the pale uniform on the left is Hermann Goering, the highest ranking Nazi on trial.

Meanwhile, there was a lot of work to be done. Much of Europe, Russia and Japan lay in ruins, and the process of rebuilding would be slow, expensive and painful. There were soldiers and refugees far from their homes and families. There were many who no longer had homes or families to go back to.

The Allied governments had failed to keep the peace after the First World War, and this time, they were determined to do better. So they set up a new international organization of countries, called the United Nations, to make sure no one started another war.

But two of these nations emerged from the war far more powerful than the others – the USA and the Soviet Union. The USA had made money by providing a lot of the equipment which won the war, and its mainland had never been bombed. The Soviet Union had surprised everyone by holding off the German army, proving itself a force to be reckoned with.

After the war, Germany was divided up into zones of occupation, as shown on this map. Later, in 1949, it was split into two countries – East Germany and West Germany. It wasn't until 1990 that Germany became a single nation again.

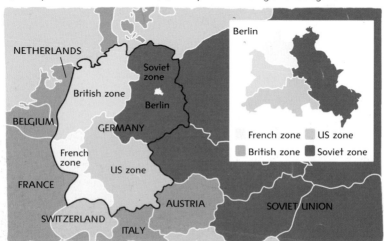

Even though the Americans and the Soviets had been on the same side, they were suspicious of each other. Soviet soldiers stayed in eastern Europe long after the war, holding on to the territories they had occupied. Winston Churchill said it was as if an "iron curtain" had come down across Europe, dividing the Soviet Union from all the countries to its west.

This was the start of the Cold War, a period of hostility between the two sides that never broke out into open warfare. Both the Soviets and the Americans developed extremely powerful atomic weapons, which had the potential to wipe out all life on earth. A real war could have meant nothing less than the end of the world.

Soviet trucks carry atomic
missiles through the streets
of Moscow in 1957.

The Second World War was the bloodiest conflict in the history of the world. Most of the 70 million people who died were not soldiers, but civilians – mothers, fathers, brothers, sisters, sons and daughters. Many of them were Asians, tortured and killed by the Japanese army. Six million of them were Jews, murdered in the Holocaust by the Nazis and their helpers.

After the war, Allied soldiers forced many German civilians to tour Hitler's concentration camps. There, they saw piles of dead Jews that the Nazis had murdered.

Some wept. Some stood and stared blankly, unable to comprehend what their leaders had done.

The Second World War left a legacy of fear, misery and mistrust. But it ended the terrifying reign of the Nazi Party, and the brutal conquests of the Japanese army.

At Nordhausen concentration camp, an American soldier watches German civilians digging graves for Jews, murdered by the Nazis.

Index

Usborne Quicklinks

You can find out more about the Second World War by going to the Usborne Quicklinks Website at www.usborne-quicklinks.com and typing in the keywords 'yr second world war'. Please note Usborne Publishing cannot be responsible for the content of any website other than its own.

White crosses mark the graves of US soldiers who died in Normandy, during the D-Day landings.